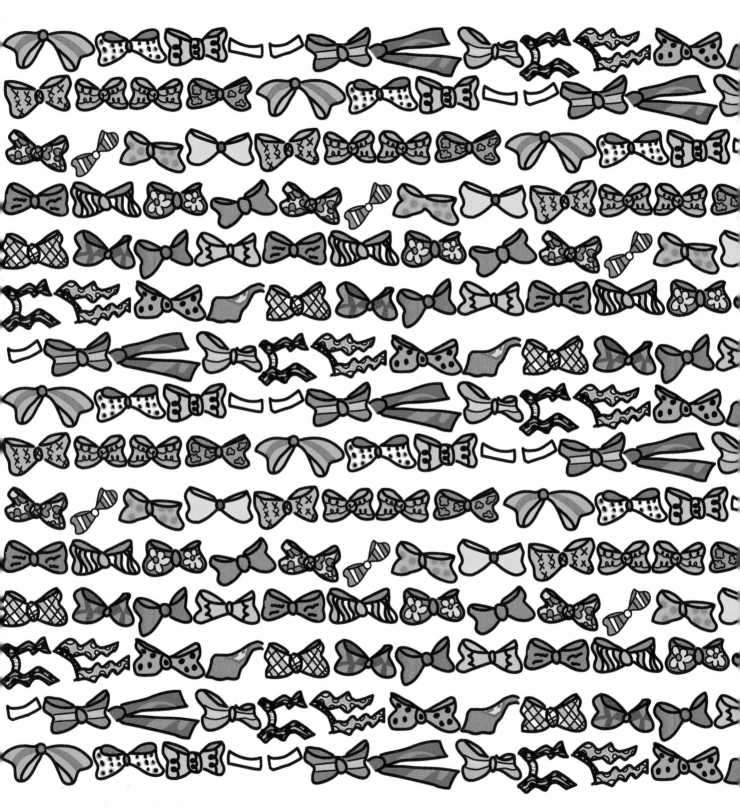

ISBNs: 978-0-9964134-0-4 (hardcover); 978-0-9964134-1-1 (ePub); 978-0-9964134-2-8 (Kindle)
Library of Congress Catalog Number: 2015941712

Printed in the United States of America
First Printing: 2015

19 18 17 16 15   5 4 3 2 1

Illustrations by Nancy Rynowecer
Book design by Jennifer Marcus Colligan
Typeset in the Georgia and Proxima Nova typefaces

Published by The BTI Press
396 Washington Street, Suite 314
Wellesley, MA 02481

www.thebtipress.com

THE BTI PRESS

To my wife Nancy—
for giving The Mad Clientist his good looks and witty personality.
And for the feedback everyone should be lucky enough to have.

Thank you to Jennifer Marcus Colligan for giving
The Mad Clientist a crucial breath of life just when he needed it.
And for edits beyond which bring out the voice and message.

The Mad Clientist's

ABCs

of

Client Service

Michael B. Rynowecer

Illustrated by Nancy Rynowecer

THE BTI PRESS

"A relationship, I think, is like a shark. You know? It has to constantly move forward or it dies."
—Alvy Singer
(Allen, Woody, dir. *Annie Hall*. 1977. Film.)

Client relationships are no different.

Client service is the fuel

driving new business and client relationships forward. I can write 22,000 words about client service—I did—see *Clientelligence: How Superior Client Relationships Fuel Growth and Profits*—but wanted to offer focused suggestions for anyone to be able to immediately boost their own client service performance, keep their client relationships moving forward, and develop more business without selling.

A is for Action

Your Actions define your clients' experience.

Your clients engage with you in hundreds if not thousands of activities over time. Your behaviors, demeanor, and approach to these actions define how your client thinks about you. Clients want to see their goals, objectives, requirements, and interests driving your actions.

Act accordingly.

 **is for Bullet**

Take one for your client.

Clients want to believe you are committed enough to stand in front of them and take the heat. This may mean you take a hit for floating a controversial idea or plan or take a non-fatal trip under a bus.

C is for Commitment to Help

Commitment to Help is the single most influential factor in any relationship. In a bacon and egg breakfast the chicken is supportive—but the pig is Committed.

Clients want pigs.

Commitment to Help is the highly subjective, personal judgment every client makes to determine if your goal is to solve a problem or bill fees. Your client's belief in your commitment is often clouded by unintended messages about rates, costs and your own interests.

D is for Devotion

Devote at least 15 minutes every day to push your understanding of your top client's industry and business.

Your accumulated knowledge is more powerful than almost any differentiator and is equally as powerful in new business development.

E is for Expectations

Clients increase their Expectations with every wonderful act you perform. Increasing client Expectations are a hallmark of a healthy relationship.

Ever-growing Expectations are the reason why good clients make you better at what you do.

F is for Feedback

You can't improve without client Feedback. Client perceptions are always different than your own self-perception. Occasionally, this perception gap works in your favor, mostly not.

Get it. Use it. Embrace it. Make client Feedback a way of life.

Feedback can change your world view and help you find completely new approaches to become truly amazing. Just look at Jimi Hendrix.

G is for Goals

Clients' Goals drive every aspect of what you do.

Your Goal is to help your client meet and exceed their Goal. If you think your client is not working towards the best Goal—your Goal is to educate your client as to why.

 **is for Hot Seat**

Your best clients will, at some point, put you in the Hot Seat. Your client will challenge your advice, and ask you the toughest questions. Your belief and compelling analytical reasoning will be put to the test.

Your client is deciding if they can rely on you. Your confidence and grace under fire will drive your relationships to new heights, and make you better at what you do. One more reason we all need good clients.

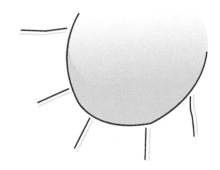
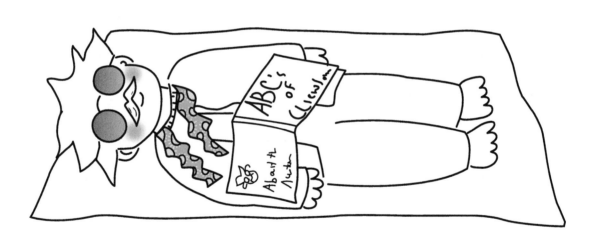

 is for Inaction

Inaction speaks much louder than words.

Clients remember acts of omission or process more than actions taken. Especially when your competitors deliver on the actions you omit.

J is for Joy

The sensation clients experience when they know the value of your service dwarfs the fee, no matter how high.

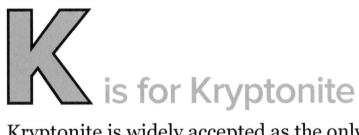
K is for Kryptonite

Kryptonite is widely accepted as the only known substance proven to render Superman vulnerable. Clients often describe the professionals best at client service as "able to leap over tall buildings in a single bound—for me."

As strong as your best performance is, beware of Kryptonite lurking in the deep recesses of client relationships. The absolute best at client service are always looking for signs of kinks in the relationship before they ever come up—lest they turn into Kryptonite—making you vulnerable almost instantly.

L is for Listen Listen Listen

Listen until it hurts. Listen with your entire body.
Listen until you understand and can integrate
what you hear into your actions.

 **is for Motion**

Make things happen. Move the mountains.
Get it done.

Continuing forward Motion and making things
happen is often hard. Very hard.

N is for No

No drives clients crazy.

Often said to clients about meeting a difficult goal, objective, budget or timeline. No is often much easier than yes.

Clients want you to get to yes. If you have to say No, what alternatives get your client to yes.

 is for Obvious

What is Obvious to you is oblivion to your client.

Articulate and share your new ideas and value you believe are Obvious for all to see.

P is for Process

Process is often more important than the outcome.

Process—especially the timing, frequency, and tone of client interface—defines how happy your client will be. Clients look to you to add knowledge and achieve a result. But, clients also want you to lighten their workload and make their life easier while delivering the result.

 is for Quality

Quality starts and ends with clients.

Clients can't see your internal quality processes ensuring a defect-free product, deliverable, or analysis. Your clients presume you have these in place.

Clients define Quality by how close you come to meeting their targeted outcome and how well you communicate as you are diligently working towards their targeted goal.

# R is for Relationship

Relationships are a state of connectedness.

Good Relationships grow, evolve, and change. Client service and communication are the fertilizers driving growth.

Stagnant Relationships atrophy and gently fade away with little fanfare, notice, or warning.

S is for Surprises

Clients hate them.

T is for a Thousand Days

You improve your client service prowess by practicing for a Thousand Days, not practicing a thousand ways. Practice superior client service long enough until it becomes muscle memory—a natural part of your daily life.

BALLOT
Write in the name and draw a portrait for your write-in-vote to count
Mad Clientist
write-in

U is for Unprompted

The overwhelming majority of C-level executives will hire you based on a single Unprompted recommendation from a peer. (An Unprompted recommendation is like a write-in vote.)

An Unprompted recommendation from your client to a peer gets you hired with no competition. Your client's Unprompted recommendation is the most powerful indicator of a superior relationship, signaling your client has made the rare emotional investment in your relationship.

 **is for Value**

The point where your client believes they have received substantially more than they pay.

Value is rarely obvious and often changes for your client as a project unfolds.

W is for W.I.T.

Whatever It Takes.

Clients want you to invest the time, energy, discipline, and grit to do Whatever It Takes to get things done.

 **is for X-Factor**

The X-Factor is a special quality unique to each and every one of your clients. Your ability to spot and understand the X-Factor enables you to craft your skills and knowledge to exceed your client's individual needs, goals, and expectations.

Y is for You

You are the most powerful component in delivering superior client service. Your actions, inactions, behaviors, and words define your client service to clients, peers, and management.

You choose to deliver superior client service and make it part of your daily life.

Z is for Zeal

Your fervor and commitment to client service shines through everything you do and every action you take.

The true zealots preach, teach, and live client service as a way of life and are ready to lead others to the promised land of superior client service.

A is for Author

Michael B. Rynowecer, as President and Founder of The BTI Consulting Group, looks at every angle of growth and strategy by starting with the client perspective. This fascination has driven him to direct, conduct, and analyze more than 14,000 one-on-one interviews with C-level executives to define their expectations, needs, priorities, preferences, hiring decisions, and opinions of the professionals with whom they work.

Michael draws on this research and his 35 years of experience to provide high-impact client feedback, brand preference and perception, business development counsel and strategic consulting to organizations who want to improve performance and drive growth.

Michael has authored more than 40 publications on all aspects of client relationships, client service, client feedback, client satisfaction, business development and business strategy.

Michael blogs at TheMadClientist.com.

I is for Illustrator

Nancy Rynowecer is a mixed media artist whose vision brought The Mad Clientist you see between these pages to life.

Nancy is drawn to organic shapes and colors found in nature combined with bits of whimsy. Her current love is mosaics, and she is a painter as well.

Nancy is also known as "Mrs. Mad Clientist".

Also by Michael B. Rynowecer

Clientelligence: How Superior Client Relationships Fuel Growth and Profits

14,000 in-depth interviews with C-level executives revealed 17 specific and unique activities driving superior client relationships.

Of these 17 driving factors:

Clients see 4 activities as scarce, delivering the absolute most value and driving hiring decisions on a continuing basis.

You can draw on these primary activities to reap substantially more business from existing clients, in good times or bad. These 4 decisive activities are:

1. Commitment to Help
2. Client Focus
3. Understanding the Client's Business
4. Providing Value for the Dollar

Clients see another 6 of these activities as the "price of admission."

These 6 activities are the minimum requirements clients set for entering into a relationship. Clients are convinced these activities are widely available from a wide group of competitors. While important, these activities fail to engender enthusiasm or generate more work. Yet this is where most people, companies, and firms focus their client-facing resources.

Clientelligence teaches you how to use these 17 activities to drive business through superior client service. Your superior relationships will deliver a steady stream of the best work—and yes, superior growth will flow.

And Coming Soon...

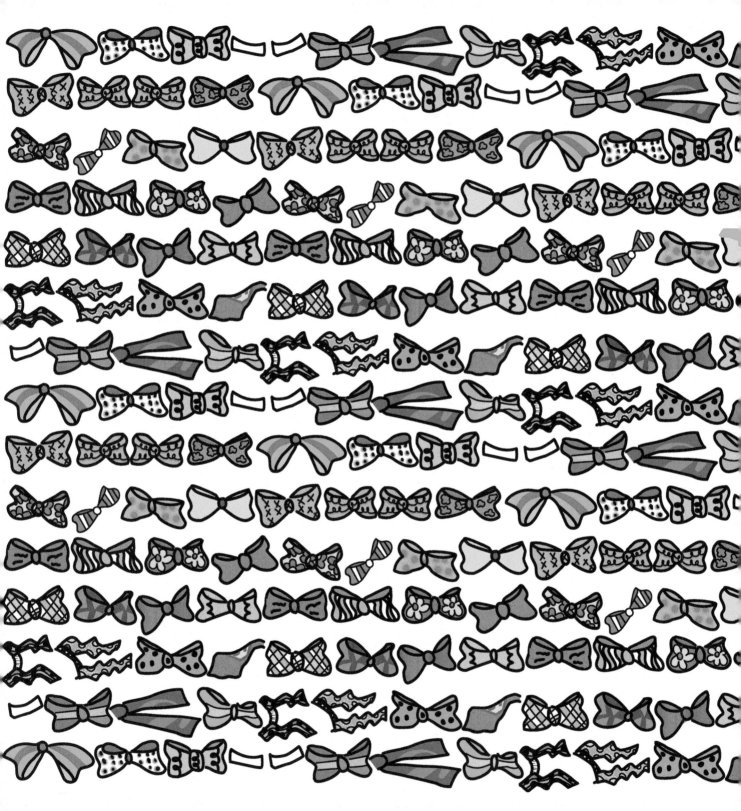

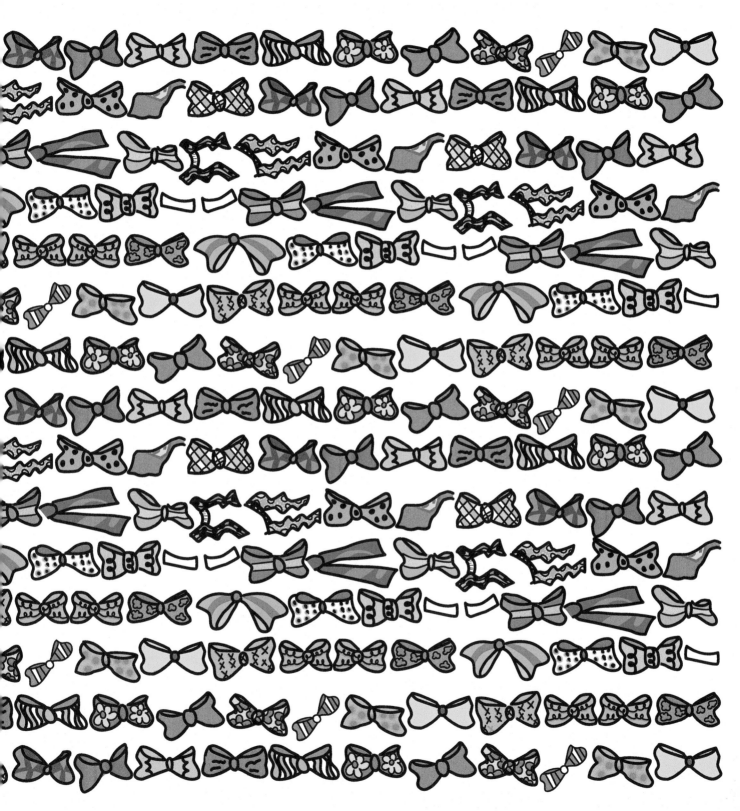

CPSIA information can be obtained at www.ICGtesting.com
Printed in the USA
BVOW11*0040120615

404340BV00001B/1/P